AR 4.7 / 0.5

D0947068

DISCOVERING

STEM at the Restaurant

STEM in the Real World

Sarah Machajewski

PowerKiDS press.

New York

Published in 2016 by The Rosen Publishing Group, Inc.
29 East 21st Street, New York, NY 10010

First Edition

Editor: Sarah Machajewski
Book Design: Mickey Harmon

Photo Credits: Cover (kitchen) Kzenon/Shutterstock.com; cover, pp. 1, 3–4, 6, 8, 10, 12, 14, 16, 18, 20, 22–24 (banner design) linagifts/Shutterstock.com; cover, pp. 1, 8, 14, 18, 20 (logo/caption box) Vjom/Shutterstock.com; p. 5 Digital Vision./Digital Vision/Getty Images; p. 7 Monty Rakusen/Cultura/Getty Images; p. 9 Jani Bryson/E+/Getty Images; p. 11 Christian Vinces/Shutterstock.com; p. 12 Warren Price Photography/Shutterstock.com; p. 13 Jiri Hara/Shutterstock.com; p. 15 ONOKY - Eric Audras/Brand X Pictures/Getty Images; p. 17 © iStockphoto.com/asiseeit; p. 19 Lew Robertson/Fuse/Getty Images; p. 21 Geri Lavrov/Photographer's Choice/Getty Images; p. 22 Monkey Business Images/Shutterstock.com.

Library of Congress Cataloging-in-Publication Data

Machajewski, Sarah, author.
 Discovering STEM at the restaurant / Sarah Machajewski.
    pages cm. — (STEM in the real world)
 Includes bibliographical references and index.
 ISBN 978-1-4994-0924-6 (pbk.)
 ISBN 978-1-4994-0926-0 (6 pack)
 ISBN 978-1-4994-0971-0 (library binding)
 1. Restaurants—Miscellanea—Juvenile literature. 2. Science—Study and teaching (Elementary)—Juvenile literature. I. Title.
 TX945.M33 2016
 647.95—dc23
                    2015006135

Manufactured in the United States of America

CPSIA Compliance Information: Batch #WS15PK: For Further Information contact Rosen Publishing, New York, New York at 1-800-237-9932

Contents

Dining Out

Where do you usually eat? You may eat at home or school, but some of the tastiest food comes from restaurants. Restaurants are businesses that serve food to people. Restaurants aren't just places to eat—they're also great places to learn about STEM.

"STEM" stands for "science, **technology**, **engineering**, and math." The skills we learn from these subjects help us understand the world around us. Restaurants are just one place we can find STEM at work.

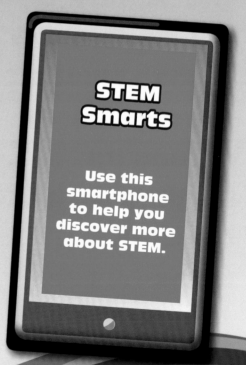

STEM Smarts

Use this smartphone to help you discover more about STEM.

This family might not know it, but STEM played a part in getting their dinner to the table.

From Farm to Table

Restaurants do a great job serving up tasty meals, but where does the food come from? Food used in restaurants comes from farms. It often has to travel a long way to get from the farm to your table.

Technology, the T in STEM, is used to **transport** food in the best way possible. Companies have invented special trucks with refrigerators that keep food cold. There are even trucks with freezers to ship meat, fish, and more. Without this special technology, certain foods would go bad before reaching restaurants.

STEM Smarts

Freeze-drying is a technology used to store food during transport. The food is frozen and then dried by removing all the ice from it. When you want to eat it, simply add water. It turns back to normal!

The food in this truck would spoil, or go bad, without technology to keep it fresh.

Growing Food

Some restaurants don't like to buy food from places that are far away. Instead, **chefs** may grow their own garden or buy food from farms in their area. This way, they know where their food comes from. This all begins with science.

Growing food starts with planting seeds. With enough sunlight and water, the seeds sprout into seedlings, or tiny plants. The tiny plants grow into fruits and vegetables that can be used for cooking. Farmers and chefs who grow their own food must understand how plants live and grow, which is an important part of life science.

Chefs in cities without a lot of open space must get creative when it comes to gardening. Some chefs grow gardens on their restaurant's roof!

STEM
Smarts

Garden tools can be as simple as a shovel or as high-tech as timed sprinklers that water gardens throughout the day.

9

Engineering a Meal

Once restaurants get food, they must turn it into something people want to eat. Chefs use machines to help them cook. This includes stoves, ovens, fryers, freezers, mixers, and more. Chefs wouldn't have these machines without engineering, which is the E in STEM.

Engineers use science and math to make machines that help us. Before the oven was invented, people cooked food over open fires. Before refrigerators, people couldn't keep food as long. If chefs didn't have these tools, their job would be much harder.

STEM Smarts

Engineers don't just make cool machines. They've created other important restaurant tools, such as pots and pans, whisks, bowls, and more.

A kitchen torch is a high-tech tool. Chefs use it to melt the top of their dish without having to put it in an oven.

The Science of Cooking

Every time a chef makes a meal, they use science to make it happen. In fact, a restaurant kitchen can feel a lot like a real-life science experiment.

Ovens and stoves are engineered to give off heat **energy**. Heat breaks down **chemicals** in food, which changes its taste and **texture**. It's what turns a hard potato into a creamy mash. Heat energy also boils water. Chefs know water is boiling when it bubbles. The bubbles are gas breaking on the water's surface. This simple science is used to cook many kinds of food, including noodles and vegetables.

STEM Smarts

Anyone who's followed a recipe knows cooking involves math. A chef must know how to measure and add half cups, whole cups, ounces, grams, pounds, and more.

Science can do wacky things to our food. The dough that made this bread contained yeast, which gave off a gas called carbon dioxide. The carbon dioxide formed gas bubbles that caused the bread to rise. When the bread was baked, the gas bubbles popped and left behind holes in their place.

POS Technology

While chefs are hard at work in a kitchen, diners are busy choosing what to eat. When they know, they place their order with a server. In modern restaurants, technology allows servers to send orders to the kitchen through a computer.

Many restaurants use a **computer program** called a point-of-sale (POS) system to tell the chefs what to make. The POS system has all the restaurant's menu choices. The server pushes the button that matches what a diner wants, and the message prints out in the kitchen.

POS technology makes it easy for a restaurant's employees to work together to make sure customers are happy and well fed.

Making Money

A lot of work goes into running a restaurant. A big part of it involves math, which is the M in STEM.

Restaurants are businesses. This means the owners want to make money. Restaurant owners use math to figure out how much money they can use to buy food. They use math skills to know how much to charge diners so they can make a **profit**. Math also tells restaurant owners how much to pay their workers and how much it costs to keep the restaurant open.

STEM Smarts

POS systems use many parts of STEM, including math. They help a restaurant total its bills, keep track of inventory, and tell owners how many people eat at their restaurant.

Handling money is a big part of
working in a restaurant.
It helps to have strong math skills.

17

Check, Please!

Every time you eat in a restaurant, you have a chance to use your own math skills. At the end of every meal, you get a bill. The bill lists everything you ordered and how much it cost. These numbers are usually added by a POS system, but many diners do their own math to make sure the bill is right.

In many restaurants, diners leave tips for the workers. The tip is usually a small percentage, or part, of the total bill. Diners use math to figure out how much the tip should be.

If you use a **calculator** to figure out a tip, you're using a tool that was engineered to help us do math. That's one way to use many STEM skills at once!

Closing Up

STEM is used even after the diners eat their meal. Dirty dishes go into a big sink or a dishwasher—tools that were invented by engineering.

Chefs see what food is left in the kitchen for the next day's meals and will come up with new ways to use it. Turning leftover food into something new is a form of food science. Finally, the restaurant's **manager** will total all the money earned. He or she uses computers to record and save the **data**. This couldn't happen without math or technology.

This manager is going through the restaurant's receipts, or pieces of paper that show something has been paid for. She's checking if the money on the receipts matches the money in the cash drawer.

Supping with STEM

Restaurants use science, technology, engineering, and math all the time. Science is used every time a chef turns food into a special dish. Technology helps restaurant workers keep track of orders. Engineering gives chefs the tools they need to create tasty meals, and math is used to total bills.

No matter where you look, STEM plays a part in helping a restaurant run smoothly. The next time you go out to eat, look around. Can you see STEM in action?

Glossary

calculator: A tool used to do math.

chef: A professional cook who makes meals in a restaurant.

chemical: Matter that can be mixed with other matter to cause changes.

computer program: A set of instructions that tells a computer or machine what task or job to perform.

data: Facts, often in the form of numbers.

energy: The ability to do work.

engineering: The use of science and math to improve our world.

inventory: All the objects contained in a restaurant's kitchen or storeroom, such as food and drinks.

manager: The person in charge of a restaurant.

profit: Money earned.

recipe: A list of food and steps needed to make a dish.

technology: The way people do something using tools. Also, the tools that they use.

texture: How something looks or feels.

transport: To carry from one place to another.

Index

Websites

Due to the changing nature of Internet links, PowerKids Press has developed an online list of websites related to the subject of this book. This site is updated regularly. Please use this link to access the list: www.powerkidslinks.com/stem/rest